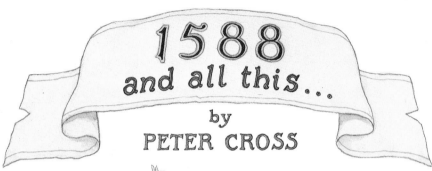

1588
and all this...

by
PETER CROSS

Life in Elizabethan England under threat of invasion by the Spanish Armada

CONTENTS ~

PAVILION
MICHAEL JOSEPH

For Kim

with acknowledgemente to
Marcus Gheeraerts the Younger (Page 4), and to Russell Ash Esquire,
who did hereby contribute to this booke various and divers
drolle ideas of a commendable and oft wondrous nature.

And speciale thankes to Peter and Bettie De Doleys,
Smithes of the parishe of Ripley, Surrey,
and purveyors of fine
soupes and pâtés.

First published in Great Britain in 1988 by
PAVILION BOOKS LIMITED
196 Shaftesbury Avenue, London WC2H 8JL
in association with Michael Joseph Limited
27 Wrights Lane, Kensington, London W8 5TZ

British Library Cataloguing in Publication Data
Cross, Peter
1588 and all this...
1. Title
828'.91407   PN6175
ISBN 1-85145-279-6

Colour origination by N.S. Graphics, London
Printed and bound by Henri Proost, Belgium

· EVENTS LEADING UP TO 1588 ·

How Drake and his sea-dogs annoyed the King of Spain

Drake's Diary

1580 *Circumnavigated the worlde...*

1585 *Plundered Spanish treasure ships*

putting the booty in

ERE YE GO
HELLO MUM
YE BOVVER BOAT
OLÉ

1586 *Disrupted International Footbowls Final outside Cadiz*

1587 *Singed the King of Spain's bearde...*

1588 *Telegramme from Liz ...*

RETURNE AT ONCE STOPPE
ALL HOLIDAYES CANCELLED STOPPE
ARMADA ON ITS WAYE STOPPE
Elizabeth R

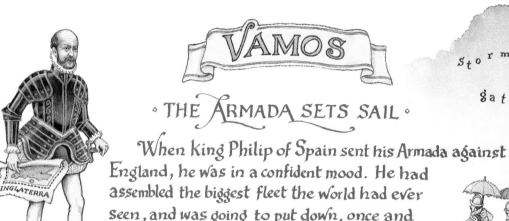

VAMOS

· THE ARMADA SETS SAIL ·

When king Philip of Spain sent his Armada against England, he was in a confident mood. He had assembled the biggest fleet the world had ever seen, and was going to put down, once and for all, the heretic Queen Elizabeth and her beer-swilling, hooligan subjects.

Storme clowdes gathering

· Spanishe storme troopes ·

And so, in April 1588, the pride of Spain's navy set sail for England. On board were soldiers, priests and many tourists on special package holidays.

Courtesy of 'JUAN'S FIGHTING SHIPS'   · UNDER STARTER'S ORDERS ·
TYPES of SHIP ~ ① Bullship ② Bulldozer ③ 'Don Quixote' (Flagship)
(Extente of available information) ④ Minotaur (minsweeper) ⑤ Papal Bully ⑥ Bullock ⑦ Worship

In a hazardous voyage across the Bay of Biscay, the tourists complained of the bad conditions. Some of the ships were unfinished, lacked basic plumbing and were often double-booked.

RUNNING REPAIRS
(ON A SANDBANK OFF CAPE FINISTERRE)

Despite the hardships, by July the Armada had sighted the coast of Cornwall,

and as the fleet prepared to sail up the Channel, the question on the lips of every Spaniard was...

"What would it be like, this England..?"

THIS ENGLAND

This royal throne of Kings, this scepter'd isle, This earth of majesty, this seat of Mars, This other Eden, demi~paradise, This fortress built for Nature for herself . . . This happy breed of men, this little world, This precious stone set in a silver sea . . . This blessed plot, this earth, this realm, this England ~ William Shakespeare Richard II Act II Scene I

Scotiæ Pars

Wallia Pars

Norfolcia

Suffolcia

Essexia

Cantuaria ✠
Cantia

Surria

Southsexia

Barnastapula

Somerseta

Hamptonia

Brightonia

Devonia

Exonia

Dorsetia

Pompeii

Corgiwallia

Falmutha

Plymutha

Vectis

·THE HOME FRONT·

This England of Queen Elizabeth was a strong, proud country, ready to do battle with anyone who dared invade her shores.

"I know I have the body of a weak and feeble woman but I have the heart and stomach of a King, and of a King of England too; and think foul scorn that... Spain or any Prince of Europe, should dare to invade the border of my Realm."

BBC

MAKE DO AND MENDE

KEEPE YE HOME FIRES BURNING

BEACON RADIO

NEWES QUEENE IN STOMACH AND HEARTE TRANSPLANT SHOCKE

SDP

Priest hole

· TUNING~IN TO THE QUEENE'S SPEECHE ·

FRONTE FOOTE FORWARDE
YOUR COUNTRY NEEDS YOU
HENRY VIII

A TUDOR RECRUITING MINIATURE

And as news of the Armada spread, hundreds of eager young recruits came forward to help defend the Realm.

McDonald's

JOIN THE NAVY AND SEE THE SEA

RN

· THE DEFENCE OF THE REALM ·

The fearsome reputation of the Spanish army did little to curb the enthusiasm of the Home Guard (*Great-great-great-great-grandad's army*). In village halls up and down the country, swains, bank clerks and veterans of the Wars of the Roses all drilled together, confident that if called upon, they could stop the Spanish war machine in its tracks.

A *Page* from the 'Home Guard Manual' of 1588 ~

Pike Exercises

YE HONOURABLE COMPANY OF PIKE & FIRELOCK

What to do if you are in a restaurant and the beacon goes up:

1 ORDER YOUR PIKE
2 PRESENT YOUR PIKE
3 ADVANCE YOUR PIKE
4 PORT YOUR PIKE
5 SHOULDER YOUR PIKE
6 DANGLE YOUR PIKE
7 CHARGE YOUR PIKE
8 JUGGLE YOUR PIKE
9 GET ON YOUR PIKE
10 SWALLOW YOUR PIKE

One of the places where the enemy might have been stopped was Tilbury. Here a barrier was built across the Thames in an attempt to deny the Armada passage into London.

YE THAMES BARRIER

London
Walton-on-the-Noze
Tilbury
The soft underbelly of the South-beaste
Armada

THE SPANISH INVASION PLAN

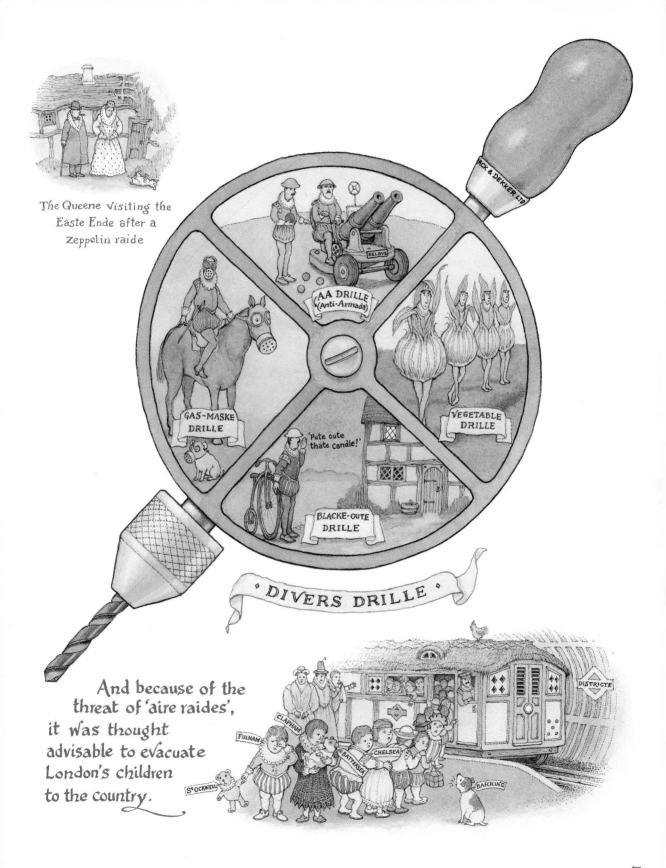

The Queene visiting the Easte Ende after a Zeppelin raide

AA DRILLE (Anti-Armada)

'Pute oute thate candle!'

GAS-MASKE DRILLE

BLACKE·OUTE DRILLE

VEGETABLE DRILLE

· DIVERS DRILLE ·

BLACK & DEKKER LTD.

RELAYE

And because of the threat of 'aire raides', it was thought advisable to evacuate London's children to the country.

St. OCKWELL

FULHAM

CLAPHAM

BATTERSEA

CHELSEA

BARKING

DISTRICTE

BE MINDFUL IN THE GARDEN

POTATOES HAVE EYES
CORN HAS EARS
WALLS HAVE SAUSAGES ETC.

· GARDEN DEFENCE ·
A Herbal Borage Balloon

· Chilton Foliat 1588 ·

DRAKE'S NAUTICAL KNOT GARDEN

· Bringe on your tommies ·

After a plot* was discovered in the Queen's kitchen garden, it was decreed that all gardens should be adequately protected and special regiments were formed.

Discovered the plot...

SECRET GARDENER

'Sir Francis Walsingham' Head of MI5

A Plymouth Hoe
A Daventry Dibber

· LEAFEATERS ·

BRIGADE OF GARDENERS

GARDEN BORDERERS

· NOSEGAYS ·

And in a popular programme of the day, a leading plantsman gave some useful tips on gardening with an invasion in mind...

YE ELIZABETHAN KITCHEN GARDEN
BBC 2, 7.40pm Wednesdaye

"If ye Spaniardes be invading this weeke-ende, then bringe in ye cowcumbers, gather ye gillyflowres, dead-heade ye daffadowndillies and hide your raspberrioes.

Remember to spraye for doodlebugs and looke-oute for Spanish fly in the onions.

Topical tippe:
Nowe's a goode time to bringe on your tommies."

Camouflage netting over the raspberries

FLITTE

seed Broadcasting

A LAND GIRL →

Digging for victory

* i.e. A vegetable plot

8

Growe Bagge

Radishe Balles

Beacon Basket

HoHo

He He

WoWo

PRIVET
KEEPE
OUTE

Clipping decoy soldiers
oute of youre fronte hedge

Digging a Ha-Ha along
the perimeter of Your property

Dog Rose

Ye Tudor rose

Ye
Boadicea
Roller

Building a 'Hans Andersen'
Shelter under the rhubarb

Planting a maze arounde
and aboute your house

Stingers

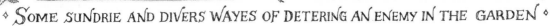

◊ SOME SUNDRIE AND DIVERS WAYES OF DETERING AN ENEMY IN THE GARDEN ◊

Detering
anemone

The defensive network of pillar-boxes and anti-tank pimples that stretched around the coast of England must have seemed a formidable sight to any invader.

A Spanish Holy Tank
('Cisterne Chapel')

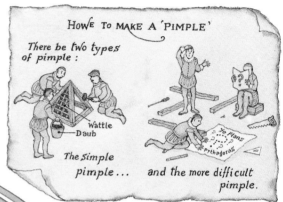

HOWE TO MAKE A 'PIMPLE'

There be two types of pimple:

Wattle
Daub

The simple pimple...

and the more difficult pimple.

Ye Plans
Pythagoras

However, the Spanish had made a study of the pillar-boxes on Gibraltar, and had developed ways of dealing with them...

The 'Pasodoble'

The Poison Pen Letter

⋄ THE PILLIBUSTER ⋄
(an early bazooka)

Adios Amigo

FROM ENGLAND

10

· Being posted ·

· On guard! ·

The few

'Poste haste'

· Camouflage ·

THE PLAN TO MAN STRATEGICALLY LOCATED PILLAR-BOXES WITH SPECIALLY
TRAINED POST OFFICE MILITIA (The Postguards).

In the event of a full scale landing, these gallant postguards were to act as front-line shock troops. The element of surprise having been gained, the postguards would then endeavour to 'holde the poste' until reinforcements arrived.

· EATING OUT ·

Life was not all to do with war. Elizabethans were great ones for enjoying themselves too.

OFF DUTY

KEEPE ENGLAND TIDY

During the Summer, many people would make for the coast where they could look out for the Armada whilst enjoying a picnic or barbecue.

Drake's Drumsticks

Batchelors Cup-a-Soupe NETTLE FLAVOUR

PRIME GUNPOWDER PATÉ

HARD TACK

ARMADA CRISPES SMOKEY BEACON FLAVOUR

SHIP'S BISCUITS Weevil and Almond Flavour BEST AFTER 1588

The lesser of 2 weevils

Peascod and Chips

A Napple

A Norange

RATION BOOKE

Sailor's take-away

No 15 "Yo Ho Ho" and No 88 "A Bottle of Rum"

HOTTE DOGGES

BARBEQUEUE HERE

SPENCER'S FAERIE LIQUIDE

for handes that washe trenchers

An outbreake of Spanish Tummy

At Court, health and beauty were very much the order of the day.

· KEEPING FIT ·

· PARA~AEROBICKES ·

The 'Raleigh' Exercise Bicycle

· MEDICINE ·

A popular nostrum →

but...

Beetles
SACK &
GUNPOWDER
with Dried
TOADE

PUSH OFF
JUNIORE
DISPIRINE

... ye alternative medicine

SCURVY
· THE FACTS ·
Can I catch Scurvy
from rubbing noses?
Is scurvy caused
by comets?
YOUR QUESTIONS
ANSWERED

① Tee Hee Bone (funny bone)   ② Tongue in cheek   ③ Titters   ④ Leg pull

· THE FOUR HUMOURS ·

· COMELINESS ·

The interpretation of patterns made by scattered toe-naile parings coulde decide the moode for the daye →

Melancholie

Merrie

After Eighty Eight Mints

TOE-NAILES

CHAPSTICKE LIP BALME

The Queen putting on her face

VENICE TREACLE

THE QUEEN'S FACIAL LOTION

· The recipe ·
White of egge, flowre, snowcem and a pinche of tippexe mixed with white elephant and beaten until frothie

MARY ARDEN ROYAL Facial Lotion

MAJORCA '87

HERBAL EIR FLOSS

ONE'S KLEENEXE WYPES EIR

EIR

Virgin Atlantic to LHR

One's bleepe & personal alarme

One's contacte lenses

HERBALDYNE GENTLE ON THE GUMS AND CAREFUL WITH THE CROWNS

One's Lavender flavoured toothepaste

One's Herbal Toothbrushe

AMERICUS EXPRESSE 15 88 ER

NUX VOMICA with extracte of cowcumber

PEPPERMINTE COMFITS

One's overnighte creame

EIR CONTACTE CLEANE for soft lenses

Contentes of the Queene's overnighte bagge

13

• RURAL PURSUITS •

Unemployment and
overcrowding in the
inner cities drove
many people to seek
recreation in the
country...

A Windmill to
be used as a
decoy should the
Spanish invade
at full tilt.

• TILTING •

← Raleigh Bicycle Clippers →

Ye Penny Farthingale

• Cycling •

• BEAR-BAITING •

• HUNTING •

• HUNT SABOTAGING •

·HOUSE HUNTING·

House prices rocketed in the '80's as everyone moved south hoping to be first to spot the Armada when it came. This created a 'North/South divide' and led to the invention of a game called 'Nine-Man Gazumping'.

PUCK & GOODFELLOW
· ESTATE AGENTS ·

A charming 9th Century one-roomed, mud-floored dwelling shared with beastes.
Offers in the region of:
28 GROATS (Fleahold)
· *Smokeless interior* · *Open conduits*
· *Carved wainscotting* · *Moat (in wet weat*

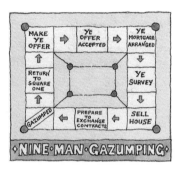

·NINE·MAN·GAZUMPING·

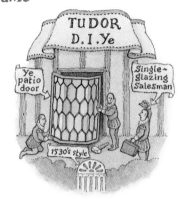

putting a small deposit on a house ▸

· A FAERIE HOUSE~CHAIN ·

• FASHION •

Keeping up appearances was important, especially during the invasion season (April to September daily except Bank Holidays).

Ruff
Cuff
Muff
Puff
A BIT OF FLUFF

MILDE, MELLOWE
Virginia Atlantic
SHIP-MATES
Ye Condome for Sailors

Sir Walter Raleigh barbecueing a potato on his new *Beacon Pipe* (*all the rage in 1588*).

FLAMMABLE ABLAZERS from GIEVES & HAWKINS
THE FLAMEBOYANT LOOKE

THE UTILITY LOOKE
THE AUSTERITY LOOKE
• For Sailors & Airmen •
BLOWE HERE
THE INFLATABLE DOUBLET
(TRIPLET ALSO AVAILABLE)
THE DE-MOBBE SUIT
NEXTE SHOPPE
GONE FOR A BURTON

• SOME RUFF STUFF •

◁ Ruffians
Ruff and tumble
cutting up ruff

RUFF & READY TO WEAR
His & Hers
SLEEPING RUFF
RUFF JUSTICE
(while stocks last)
'RUFFLES'
Disposable Ruffs
INFLATABLE
RUFF
Ruff time

Ruff measure

◊ TUDOR T.V. and Radio ◊

After a hard day's work, the nation would settle down to an evening's entertainment.

GRAVESENDERS
BBC I : 7·30, *Tuesdaye & Thursdaye*

CALL MY RUFF
BBC II : 8·00, *Thursdaye*

CHANNEL IV NEWES
7.00 , *Mondaye to Frydaye*

DONASTY
BBC I : 8·10, *Saturdaye*

Ye ARCHERS
BBC RADIO IV : 1·40, *Daily*

MIDWEEKE SPORTE SPECIAL ~ ITV : 10·30, *Wednesdaye*

'Thou can'st not be serious'

Complaining about the bad service

TABLE TENNIS

THISBEE

NINE MAN'S MORRIS

Ted Drake · Plymouth & Hoe Albion

FOOTEBOWLS

But when duty called...

CONFRONTATION

◇ THE ARMADA SIGHTED ◇

On 29ᵗʰ July, the Armada was sighted off Cornwall. All England was on stand-by as beacons were lit up and down the country.

29ᵗʰ July

31ˢᵗ July

3ʳᵈ August

SOME DIFFICULTIES CONCERNING BEACONS

Ye False Alarum

FALSE BEACONS
Developed by the Spanish as a means of decoye

PUTTING OUT THE BEACONS

Ye Fire Brigade preparing to go to a blaze

A Larum bell

Trunk & hose

Ding-a-dong, ding-a-dong, the Fireman's song.
"We go to blazes big and small,
Bonfire or beacon, give us a call;
With a hey nonny nonny etc..."

Collecting foame to fille fire extinguishers

18

THE NEWᵉ, FULLᴵᴱ AUTOMATICKE *BELISHA* SAFETᴵᴱ BEACON

⬩ Ye *BEACON* COLOURᵉ CODE ⬩

RED ALERTE
STOP what you are
doing ~ to your postes!
Invasion imminent and
probable within 12 dayes.

AMBER ALERTE
PROCEED with
caution. Invasion expected
and possible within nexte
2 monthes.

GREENE ALERTE
GO aboute your
normale business.

what's
a lerte?

· AN ARMADA LISTENING~POSTE ON BEACHY HEAD ·

· KEEPING TRACK OF THE ARMADA ·

Along the south coast of England, Postguards plotted the course of the Armada as it sailed up the Channel.

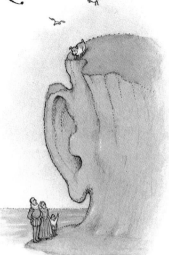

Lughole in Cornwall where they first heard about the Armada.

INSIDE A LISTENING·POSTE
Conditions were deliberately cramped so that the occupant would not fall asleep while on duty.

EARWEGO EARWEGO EARWEGO

Queen Elizabeth in the 'Ops Roome' at Nonsuch Palais

· LISTENING FOR THE ARMADA IN PLYMOUTH SOUND ·

Sound waves travel a long distance through water and it was thought that it might be possible for landsmen to get within earshot of the passing Spanish.

Earshot

THE FIGHTING

·ENGLAND EXPECTS·

As the English fleet prepared to do battle with the Armada, Drake made his now legendary comment: 'England expects that there will be plenty of time to finish the game and fight the Spaniards on the beaches.'

·DUCKS AND DRAKES·

Drake 'knocking up' with his captains before the first rubber with Spain

ENGLISH FLIPPERS SPANISH FLIP-FLOPS

Drake's Secret Weapon (See p. 26-27)

In the fighting to come, it soon became evident that the new English flipper was more than a match for the Spanish flip-flop.

· THE PRIVATEERS ·

The privatisation of the Navy in 1587 led to some interesting new designs...

A bunch of 'Sea Fives'

THE NOAH'S ARQUEBUS

· An improvised troopᵉ transportᵉ used to carry · · freshᵉ men to the fronte ·

A A small bark

23

DOG·FIGHTS IN THE CHANNEL

Grapeshotte

ye phoney war

Running
agrounde

WADDINGTON'S
DOVER PATROLE

Vapour trails from Drake's Sea-Dogges as they
engage the Armada off the coaste of Dorset

Ye Commemorative
Armada

Engagement Ringe

· THE BATTLE OF 'JEUX SANS FRONTIERES' ·

Dogged by the English and exhausted by the long voyage, the Armada put into Calais. Whilst the Spanish vessels grazed peacefully in the harbour, Drake deployed his secret weapon ~ the fire·box. In the ensuing confusion, the frightened Spanish ships panicked, causing a terrible stampede.

MARACAS.
Deadly at close range

Put oute Your Tim...
5,000 Make a pinna...
25,000 Make a Man...
o'war

• HOW THEY LINED UP •

ADIOS

◦ THE END OF THE ARMADA ◦

"There will be no Armada"

Before the Armada could re-group, the weather took a turn for the worse. Strong winds blew the ill-fated Spanish northwards and many galleons came to grief on the rocky shores of Scotland and Ireland.

15 SEPT. 1588 ◦ Ye Weather Forecaste ◦
From the Tudor Weather Centre

"If you're looking oute for the Armada this weeke-ende, then there coulde well be ships coming ashore off the north of Scotlande, and off Northern Irelande by nexte weeke.

If we looke at the satellite picture for noone todaye then, we canne see this area of lowe pressure driving the Armada northwardes, and bringing with it sundry zephyrs and tempestes.

The outelooke for nexte weeke: Continuing unsettled with, hopefully, zephyrs gusting to gale force by Tuesday.

That's it then, and a very goode nighte."

LOWE

LOWE/HIGHE
POLLEN COUNTE

· HIGHE TIDE TABLE ·

London Bridge	3.16 am	3.39 pm
Dover	12.18 am	12.47 pm.

SUN RISES ~ Morning
SUN SETS ~ Evening
MOON RISES ~ Evening
MOON SETS ~ Morning

LIGHTING-UP TYME

Around the beacons yesterdaye ye Lunch-time reportes		
Penzance	64 18	Faire
Plymouth	61 16	Foule
Swanage	59 15	Nebulous
Bognor	61 16	Mizzle
Eastbourne	57 14	Watty
Margate	55 13	Flurries
Clacton	– –	Teeming
Skegness	50 10	Deluge

Around the worlde approx. 3 months ago		
Azores	84 29	Sunne
Cadiz	79 26	Balme
Lisbon	79 26	Rainebowe
Nombre de Dios	82 28	Sizzle
New Sidcup	91 33	Drouth
Rome	84 29	Phewe
Virginia	77 25	Whata
Zanzibar	88 31	Scorcher

Survivors of the shipwrecks leave their mark in the Highlands...

· THE VICTORY PARADE ·

When news of the Armada's demise reached London, there was much rejoicing and peeling of bells. A grand victory parade was held and the Queen herself took the salute.

And so the threat of invasion had passed, and after the humiliation of 1066, England was able to enjoy the first of her many 'Finest Hours'. It was an experience that was to see her through similar crises in the centuries to come and served notice to any foreign power that had its eyes on this green and pleasant land...

YE NATIONAL TRUSTE

NO INVADING!
ALSO PLEASE AVOIDE LEAVING LITTER LIGHTING FIRES AND DAMAGING PLANTS

1988 AND NOW ALL THIS...
CHANNEL TUNNEL STARTED